Business Process Re-engineering: An Improvement Approach to improve Business Performance

(c) 2012 Smartspeed Consulting Limited. All rights reserved.

Disclaimer:

The author of this book has tried to present the most accurate information to his knowledge at the time of writing. This book is intended for information purposes only. The author does not imply any results to those using this book, nor are they responsible for any results brought about by the usage of the information contained herein.

No part of this book may be reprinted, electronically transmitted or reproduced in any format without the express written permission of the author.

Table of Contents

Cutting Through The Confusion	4
Part One - The Engine	9
Brand and Value	11
Mapping	23
Key Performance Indicators	35
Handovers	44
Sales Intake and Regulation	53
Discipline and Routines	62
Regulation of Resources	70
Improving Your Processes	79
Part 2 - Fuel for the Engine	99
Getting Things Moving	107
Experiment and Make Progress	113
Prioritisation	120
5 Why – Root Cause Problem Solving	126
Simplifying Job Roles	129
Summary	136
The Next Steps	139
Compilation of Action Points	143
Links and Resources	152
About Giles Johnston	154
Smartspeed's Contact Details	155

Cutting Through The Confusion

This book is a tool to help you find some quick improvement approaches for your business. It is not designed to be the gospel on business improvement. It is designed to be a huge kick start.

There is so much information available through the Internet, books and colleagues that it can sometimes be difficult to work out where to start. There are so many methodologies and systems available to you that you would be forgiven if you found the whole prospect daunting.

This book is a remedy to the confusion. The information and recommended actions are taken from my experience. The information is intended to be highly practical, ideas that can be implemented immediately and usually at low cost. The sections are based upon my practical experience of generating fast results for clients.

After about five years of delivering improvement projects for my clients I started to see patterns emerging. Different businesses with different problems, but similar needs and solutions were starting to emerge. Due to the variety of projects the solutions were all different, but nonetheless there were common parts that were implemented. Pulling these common elements out and using them in a more controlled 'holistic' fashion generated even better results for my later clients and these building blocks form the basis of this book.

Two parts

The first part of this book covers the main building blocks that I mentioned above, the second part of the book looks at some of the other tools that I have found to be beneficial in making improvement activities work even better. If part one is the engine then part two is the fuel.

As you read the chapters you will most likely recognise some of the principles, especially if you have read books on Lean and Six Sigma. This will help you, but don't worry if you haven't. The whole idea of the book is to help you in making improvements and not get lost in philosophical battles of what is the right way to improve a business. There are many businesses who get on and improve - they do it naturally - it's part of what they do. Other businesses look to these businesses and try to pull apart what they do and try to emulate their systems. I don't think that there is a perfect way to improve. I do think that some of the systems work well, but there are also some principles sitting behind the systems that will always work. The hard part of making sustainable changes happen is contained in two tasks:

One: Maintaining an ongoing conversation in the business about improvement.

Two: Continuing to try new ideas and plugging away until improvement occurs.

Many businesses want a perfect improvement plan and get nowhere. Others pick a direction (and goals if appropriate) and work out the best plan to their knowledge and get going. They refine their ideas along the way and by chipping away they soon arrive at a brilliant destination. Sometimes this happens quickly, and sometimes it takes longer. There are so many variables present within a business that working out and predicting the precise plan can be nearly impossible. So, keep aiming for better and keep going.

Structure

Each section of the book has a number of points and

always concludes with some action points. The sections aren't designed to be formulaic; the idea is that you understand the principle of the section and then work out how best to do something similar in your business. As you read through the text you may possibly see a larger improvement approach lurking in the background. If you know how to expand upon the approach great, come up with a plan and go to it. If you don't recognise the approach then don't worry, that's why I wrote this book. Don't spend ages getting lost in theory, review the practical aspect of each section, come up with a plan for your business and then get on and do something about it.

Also, don't worry about the work involved. Get a team in your business to work on these ideas, engage in discussion and exploration and then try some ideas out. You will almost certainly be improving your business just from having some meaningful conversations. There are so many businesses out there that hope that the next system will be the one that gives them the answers. The systems don't have answers - you and your team do. Use the ideas in this book to develop your own conversations and don't worry if the approach gets messy. Keep moving forwards and keep improving, that's the only formula.

Action steps

- Read the rest of the book!

- Start an ongoing conversation with your colleagues about improvement.

Part One - The Engine

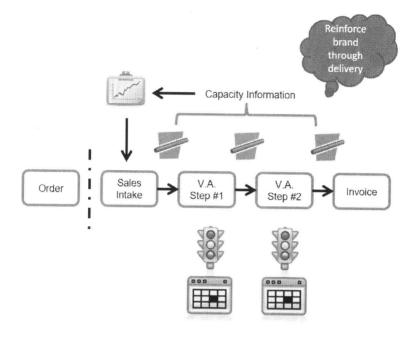

Brand and Value

Know what is important to the business and to the customer so as to create a direction for making improvements.

Key Performance Indicators

Drive the performance of your business through having the right information at the right place at the right time.

Handovers

Remove the delays and mistakes between stages for big results.

Sales Intake
Ensure that the way that you accept work doesn't cripple the business.

Regulation
Optimise your resources by making sure things are happening the right way and the control of your capacities.

Routines
Improve the discipline / regimen in the workplace for repeatable results.

Processes
Find the best way to do your work.

Brand and Value

Value

Value is a term that often confuses businesses. Value is what your customer is willing to pay for.

If you have followed any of the books around Lean then you will be aware of the balancing act in every business between value and waste.

- Value is what your customers want.

- Waste is everything else that you do to satisfy their needs / wants.

In many businesses this distinction leads into how profits are generated in the business. If the market forces are strong enough then reducing the wastes present in your business may be the only way to increase your profitability.

The key point I want to get across here is that by understanding what value you offer your customers you will be in possession of some simple principles that can help guide your improvement activities.

The objective of this section of the book is to define a compass for your business so that when improvement opportunities are discovered you can consider them against this compass and decide what action needs to be taken. Also, if there are no obvious opportunities and you find yourself in limbo then this compass will help you to decide where you need to focus your efforts.

If this is new to you and you are trying to discover your value proposition then you will need to realise that it will be something really basic, something a ten year old child will be able to comprehend. There are many other things that we do as a business that are impressive, sexy or clever. In a lot of cases our customers aren't that bothered. They just want the end result or product. Don't feel too depressed when you strip your business down to its value proposition, you still get to do everything else, but perhaps you will change how much of each activity you will do going forwards.

Think of your value - what do you offer?

- Do you mow lawns?

- Do you cut metal?

- Do you assemble microwaves?

- Do you design buildings?

Keep thinking about your business until you get to that 'Aha!' moment when you realise that most of the things you do in your business don't contribute to the value that your customers want.

Brand

The impression you leave upon your customers is your brand. Your operational brand is the way that you deliver your products and services and the way that your customers feel about that experience. Brand is so much more than a logo or your stationery or your website. Your brand is enforced or betrayed with every interaction with your customer. By understanding where you are now and where you want to be you can define a path for your improvement activity to take place.

Hopefully you will have some idea of how you would like to be perceived, this is your 'ideal brand'.

Voice of the customer

A great place to start in identifying your own brand is to understand what your customers think of you. In many cases there is an ongoing dialogue between you and your customers and suppliers so tapping into this is the best place to start. Remember the customer will see your business differently to you and uncovering this distinction is of paramount importance to establish your current brand.

If your customers aren't speaking to you then that is possibly a sign that they are not happy with you and aren't saying anything. Most healthy relationships will lead to some dialogue. You may have received complaints or unofficial grumbles. You may have been awarded prizes. Every contact with the customer tells both parties something about the other. Compile a list of the feedback you get and create a view from the customer. This is your 'actual brand'.

Ideal brand versus actual brand

In many cases there will be a gap between the ideal and actual brands that you have defined. This gap gives you a guide to what needs to change in your business.

This is also a great time to review and update your ideal brand. Align the brand with the mission or goals of your business. There might be other things that have come up from your customer feedback that could be incorporated – things you had never considered before.

The intention of doing this is to help build our compass. To provide decision making and guidance when opportunities for improvement come flooding in.

Our focus

How we look at our business affects what we do with it. When we use our simple top level view of our world (our value [what] and our brand [style]) we get a simple tool to apply to make our business great. If we don't have a focus then all of the opportunities for change will look good. We need to be able to discriminate and be selective. Some of the improvements will make a big impact on our brand whilst others will not. Some will make a marginal improvement to our ability to create value for our customers and other will give a huge boost.

Every improvement has its place, but when time is limited we need to be able to make swift decisions about which of the options available are the best to pursue. If time and need allows we may get round to resolving some of the options that were in second or third place when we evaluated them. The choice has to be made however to make the most important and most effective changes first.

Once we have effectiveness then we can look at efficiency. Most of the practical sections of this book are aimed at increasing effectiveness. Some of these changes however will improve efficiency by default, so don't worry, efficiency is also covered.

Principles for change

Now it is time to distil the brand awareness and value insights into some principles for change. This requires you (and your team) to come up with some simple statements that can help guide your thoughts during the upcoming activities. This set of statements will become your compass.

Don't worry about getting these statements perfect the first time round, your thoughts will most likely change as this period of change takes effect, but it is a great place to start.

An example may help you get started:

If you want to be seen as the 'go to' people for a certain manufactured part but you find out that your late deliveries and unclear e-mails are causing distress for the customer you may wish to have some of the following principles:

- E-mails are to be standardised, simple and clear.

- All steps in our order conversion process are to start on time and to finish on time.

- All order problems are to be flagged up at a daily meeting.

- Admin tasks are to be minimised.

- Value adding tasks are to be supported to reduce stoppages.

- All phone calls are to be answered within three rings.

I hope you get the idea now. Write down a handful of statements for future use.
When you are generating improvement ideas these statements can help you prioritise which actions are the most important in order for you to live your brand.

Summary

If we get a handle on what our business creates from a **value** point of view, and combine this with an honest look at how we are performing, our **brand**, then we can create a compass for our business' improvements. Improvement doesn't need to be guesswork and the actions that we need to take can become self evident.

Action steps

- Determine what value your business creates for its customers. Keep this as a focus for your improvements; we want to spend as much time on value adding work as possible.

- Compare your ideal brand with your current brand, where you want to be and where you are. All your changes need to help you move from your current brand to your ideal brand.

- Define some statements / principles for change to help you achieve your ideal way of working. Your changes need to help you adhere to your ideal brand and help your business to spend more time on value adding.

These three items will be your compass for change. Reflecting upon these from time to time will help you to ensure that your efforts are moving you in the right direction.

Example: Knowing your real brand

One of my clients had a problem with how their customers saw them. The client wanted to be the supplier of choice in a certain industry. Technically they were very good, but delivery wise it was a totally different story. Most of the orders were delivered late and it took a long time to process the orders. The client even had letters of complaint that they could show me. This was a good sign we decided - their customer still wanted to work with them (as they could have gone quiet and found an alternative supplier).

The feedback from their customers gave some immediate pointers as to what brand they wanted the business to be and we used this to identify the gap in their actual brand. We also considered their value proposition and identified the chunks of the business that were critical and those that were not. This was not to devalue any part of the business it was to put things in perspective so that this business could become what they needed it to become.

There was no point in improving something that didn't matter; we needed to find a way to use those resources more effectively.

Based on both of these conversations we also came up with some principles to keep us on track. The most profound of these was the simple statement 'we will start all of our orders on time'.

There were additional conversations that took place over the next couple of weeks within my client's business, topics that we will discuss in the following sections. But, with this one discussion this particular company found that their on-time delivery performance increased by around 40 percentage points during the following month.

Knowing where you are and what you need to be in order to get what you want is an important first step.

Mapping

The quickest way to get improvement happening in your business is to draw a map.

There are many different approaches to process mapping including flow charts, value stream maps and swim lanes. Feel free to choose whatever you prefer, to get down on paper the key steps in your processes. Getting a group of people to work out the steps, agree upon the sequence, and to understand the gripes that are held about the process (as it stands) are the objectives for this section.

Don't get hung up on the method. Boxes with arrows and scribbled notes will do just fine!

Identify the processes

The first step is to work out what we need to map. There are three main types of process. The first is our order conversion processes – the processes required to convert something into something else.

If you work in manufacturing this would be the process of converting your customer orders into a despatched product, if you are an online retailer this would be the process of turning an order into a despatched item, if you are a gardener this could be turning overgrown gardens into beautiful gardens.

The second type of process is for projects, which may include new product introductions. Usually businesses will look at the main conversion processes and then get really stuck when an oddball project is unleashed into the business. Knowing how you handle these projects and deliver the results in a slick fashion is certainly worth reviewing and improving.

The third type of process to map is administrative processes. Usually these are supportive in nature to the first two types of process. Knowing the types of resources required and how they feed into the other processes can add invaluable information into the decision making when choosing what improvements to progress later on.

The remainder of this book will be referring to the first type of map - the order conversion process as this is where many businesses find the greatest immediate benefit. The same ideas and techniques can be applied to the other two processes, by repeating the steps in this book with those processes as the focus instead.

Define the steps

Once you have assembled your team to review the

processes you will need to agree some ground rules with the team, usually:

- There is no criticism of any questions.

- Everyone gets a chance to speak.

- All ideas are accepted on face value until later on.

You will also need to agree on where the process starts and ends.

Once you have everyone playing nicely and the start and end is agreed, it is time to start working your way through the process, step by step. If you get multiple answers for the routes through the process then take them all, it may get confusing but you are possibly looking at some immediate opportunities for improvement. Multiple routes and rework loops may seem confusing at this stage, but the wealth of information that you are receiving will be useful later on.

At this point accept the fact that the mapping is confusing (if it is) and carry on, the later steps will help to straighten this all out.

Obstacles

Whilst you are mapping there might be obstacles that get brought out in the discussion, these are fine, just don't lose them. They might appear to cloud the overall mapping process and with time being a finite resource we want to make sure that the maximum amount of time at this stage is spent on recording the steps. Two ideas on how to best use these 'observations' are to use sticky notes to keep a reference of the obstacle next to the step that it was identified against, or record it on a big list somewhere for future consideration. Just don't lose them!

Another issue that might get raised (and if it doesn't then you should raise it) is that of rework. Rework cycles in a process are not uncommon and are a symptom of the process steps not being adequate earlier on. This is another opportunity for improvement right in front of you. Rework loops are definitely worth recording whilst going through the mapping exercise.

If the people taking part have facts and figures to go along with the rework loops then even better. By understanding the rework loops you will be able to work out how effective your process is for doing what you do 'right first time', this yield information can be very useful for monitoring and managing rework.

Gripes

Throughout the mapping process there will be questions raised and gripes made. Although we don't want the mapping to get put on the back burner in favour of a slanging match, it is worth recording the gripes. Some agreement between the team members is advisable, guidelines could include:

- Don't make the gripes personal.

- Make it process based.

- Be objective.

- Don't rely on guesses – facts only.

- No solutions, only observations.

Keep this list for future work. In my experience there is usually a split in the list. One third is right on the money and the issue needs to be addressed without delay. One third will be in a grey area and will need to be fleshed out and understood better before a resolution can be determined. The other third will be way off the mark, but a great opportunity for education about how other parts of the business operate. Encourage the gripes to be shared and don't lose the list. Remedying the list of gripes over time will help build momentum in the business.

The 'because of' statement

When you have a completed map of your process a good technique to use is the 'because of' statement. By starting at the end of the process you can work your way backwards through the process linking each step with 'because of'. If the statement makes no sense then you have an ideal opportunity to review how the two are linked together, at best you may find some redundant steps that you can remove immediately. For example you might run through your process in reverse and say:

- Last operation – 'despatch of products'

- Joining statement - because of

- Previous operation – 'products packed'

This example makes sense and has a logical flow to it. If there is no logic to the flow then it is worth checking that there are no steps missing, or that a step should be there in the first place.

Immediate ideas

When you (and your team) stand back from your handiwork and look at your map, and the list of gripes, there will probably be a number of immediate improvements that spring to mind. Gaining momentum is a force to take advantage of. If there is momentum in the group to do something that will have an obvious benefit, is low cost and low risk to implement then let them do it. We will review tracking improvements later in this book, but making positive changes to how the business operates is the goal of this book. It is sometimes worth starting with things that are not the top priority just to get some momentum going, when this happens just make sure that your top priority is primed so that it gets done second (but done in a far better way now that the team is warmed up!).

Delete / merge

Some of the steps in the process may be removed from just identifying the full array of steps during this mapping stage. If it makes sense then do it.

Some steps in the process can be merged to save a gap between steps – if these are obvious then make these a priority also.

The future

The following sections of this book are going to look at improving the way that your business operates, and part of that is looking at the map that remains after doing the above couple of actions. There is the opportunity here to completely re-engineer the way that you do things. The subsequent sections of this book will help you to do that in specific ways, but there is nothing like asking yourself the question 'if we were to set up this process again, from scratch, how would we do it?'

You might want to leave this idea with the team over the next few days / weeks. You may come up with a completely new way of working.

Think it over, don't worry if you don't come up with any ideas – the next few chapters will help you to move up a gear or two without complete re-design.

Summary

Creating a map doesn't need to be hard, just get a team together and start drawing out the steps of the process as they occur, warts and all! Don't worry if it gets messy and there are problems with the process, getting the map drawn is rarely a straightforward affair. Keep a log of the problems people face and use your map as a springboard into improvement.

Action steps

- Identify your processes.

- Get your team together and list all of the steps and agree their sequence.

- List the gripes and obstacles that the process faces / creates.

- Check the process steps with the 'because of' statement.

- Act upon the immediate ideas.

- Delete and merge steps that are obvious.

- Consider ideas for a total overhaul – as if you started all over again.

Example: Finding the real route

A client of mine was complaining that the length of time it took to fulfil their orders was too long. This business was involved in the manufacturing of relatively simple components, but they seemed to deliver late for most of the time. I was asked to find out where the problem was within the manufacturing process. Concerned that the problem was not primarily in manufacturing I asked the client to extend their scope into the sales order processing part of the business. Reluctantly they agreed and we created a map from the very start of the sales order through to the despatched articles.

Nearly two thirds of the lead time was taken up by the administration of the paperwork before it even got onto the shop floor! Over the years the business had grown and personnel had changed. Along with these changes were minor modifications as to how the paperwork was being handled. Fast forward five years and you had a business process punctuated with in trays, job sharing and a lack of seeing what the full picture was. Orders would sit for days waiting for the next two minutes worth of activity to take place.

The full map of the business' order fulfilment system was recorded and there were a number of opportunities that were clearly available for the manufacturing element of the business to deal with. The point I am stressing here is that things may look OK, but if we don't get some facts then we may well be kidding ourselves. When we map a system or a process then we can get clear about how things work or don't work.

Needless to say my client was quite taken aback when they saw the map and just how muddled and confused the process had become. The transformation wasn't difficult, it just needed everyone who was in the process to step back and review the map and realise how they could work better as a team in the order administration functions. The sales order processing/ purchasing function now takes less than 10% of the full order lead time and deliveries are made on time for more than 95% of the time.

Key Performance Indicators

There are many texts available on how to implement key performance indicators (KPIs) into businesses and many of them are great. When I travel around different businesses one of the things that I see occurring is information that is being recorded but not used to help the business change direction (as and when appropriate). This section of the book is going to look at how we can implement KPIs that are meaningful, simple and that drive performance.

Cause and effect

For ease KPIs can be put into two camps, those at cause and those at effect. Most KPIs that are used in business are at effect. They include profit, on time delivery and customer satisfaction. When an indicator is at cause they can be similar in nature but located at different places, or they can be entirely different measures. For example we may want to achieve 100% on time delivery rates. To work out if we are going to deliver on time we may want to know if the release of the paperwork from the office into production was on time. If we are able to achieve an on time completion further up stream in the process then we will most likely have the best chance of completing (in this case) the production order on time.

Some of the most interesting KPIs can be measured in a digital fashion as opposed to the usual analogue scale. For example if you were running a purchasing department you could measure the number of orders placed that day (analogue) but that may not tell you what you need to know. A more interesting measure (or question) could be 'have all of the orders that needed to be placed today been placed?' This would give us a 'yes' or a 'no'. We could measure this over the day (0% or 100% achievement) or over a week (each day would be worth 20% in a 5 day working week). If you got a handful of 'no' responses then you could probably see a problem facing the business in a few days / weeks / months as materials or other purchased items don't arrive on time for the business to use.

If we measure some of our processes at cause then the effects will be more expected, rather than a pleasant or unpleasant surprise.

If you are still wondering about how to approach this in your business then consider the dashboard of a car. If you are about to take a journey and you know where you need to be, and at what time, then on-time delivery is our main KPI of success. In the car you are equipped with a number of 'gauges' that can help you measure your progress. As you drive the car you would probably be able to see your fuel level, your engine speed (revs), your car's speed, the current time and distance already travelled. Combinations of this information would let you have some indicators that would inform you as to the progress of your journey. If your fuel level is dropping quicker than expected and your engine speed is high then you may decide to change gears. If your speed is low and your distance travelled is less than expected then you may choose to exercise the option of speeding up.

When your KPIs are at cause you have a chance to do something about the effect. When your KPIs are only at effect you only get to read a story about what happened.

Appropriate indicators

At different levels in a business the need for information changes. When you are designing your KPIs you need to make sure that you have taken into account the different requirements and understood what is appropriate information. The needs of the Financial Director will be different to the needs of the Team Leader and so your mix of KPIs should be able to answer the question 'will everyone in the business be able to understand what direction we are travelling in?'

Direction of travel

One of the most useful functions of a KPI is to determine the direction of travel. This may be an averaged form of the KPI but helps to keep context in the business should you experience a blip. Some days the performance might be amazing and other days awful. Using a summarised version of the KPI will help you to determine the trend and work out the most appropriate course of action. If you have ever suffered from knee jerk reactions in the workplace previously then this can help to prevent them by letting everyone look at the bigger picture. The severity of a blip should be understood by the organisation. A blip in an operating theatre is much different to a blip at the checkout of a supermarket in terms of consequence. Appropriate responses should be determined before the blip is encountered.

Stimulating appropriate action

You may want to bind some of the key performance indicators with actions. If an indicator drops below a certain level you may have some predefined actions that take place. If the trend behaves in a certain way then a different course of action may be defined. For example, from a purchasing perspective - one poor result means speak to the supplier, five poor results means escalating the problem to the supplier development team.

Pre-defining actions around KPIs can help to reduce time required by management / directors working with lower level issues.

The re-deployment of resources is an interesting use of KPIs and this will be touched on in a later section.

Summary

KPIs can be enormously useful to a business and help to quickly change activities / behaviours to ensure that the right results are achieved. Having a split of KPIs between causal and 'at effect' indicators will give the best representation of the business and enough manoeuvring room to improve the results if they are not looking favourable.

Action steps

- Review the process map you have been working on and define the key steps in the process where specific achievements would allow improvement of the final results. For example, "paperwork completed on time at the sales order processing stage".

- Identify the 'digital' tasks that need to be included. These are the 'yes' or 'no' questions that can help to decide if a function has operated in accordance with its purpose in the business.

- Decide how the information that you can gain from these KPIs could be used and manipulate its form until a meaningful measure is achieved. For example if you were recording the lead time through a production facility you may have some interesting information but it wouldn't give you any guidance as to how to improve the performance. If you then looked at the stages of production and were able to use the same data to determine adherence to stages of production then you would create an exception report that would tell you where and when to distribute your resources so that on time order fulfilment could be achieved.

- Review the list of KPIs and consider the people and functions in your business to see if a concise but all encompassing list has been achieved. If the list looks too long then you may need to trim or consolidate some measures. There is no right or wrong answer when doing this. If it's right for your business then it's right.

- Pre-define the corrective actions that need to take place when specific KPI performances have been 'breached'.

Example: Knowing the standard is essential

One of my clients in the service sector was struggling to cope with the volume of paperwork that needed to be processed in one of the early parts of their order conversion process. My initial thoughts were to find what was unnecessary and delete the requirement altogether. Unfortunately my client had already done this and what they were left with was deemed essential.

What I did find out after a little bit of digging was that no one had properly spoken to that department about the problem (they were busy - so what?), so we invited them to find out what we were doing and then asked them some questions so we could learn about their particular issues. I explained the knock on effect of their paperwork being completed later than required with regards to the completion of projects. I then explained the car dashboard analogy from this section of the book and asked them how long it should take them to process the paperwork through their department.

Before our conversation the paperwork was taking just over seven working days, and I was hoping we could negotiate a standard of three days to work to. The person in question offered us one day. Surprised,

I asked him what help he would need from the management team to make this happen. "None" he replied. Still taken aback I asked him how long it would take to make this happen, I was expecting two weeks to be his reply. "From tomorrow" was his actual reply. We agreed upon this offer he had made and included his new 'lead time' metric into our mix of key performance indicators.

True to his word the lead time was only one day from that point onwards. By measuring the rest of the performance measure and making the necessary daily adjustments this client's on time delivery performance soared. By just being clear about the standards we needed to work to sorted out the main problem area of the business' performance. By having the full range of metrics the senior management of the business were able to manage it appropriately and their customers became a lot happier.

Handovers

Within most businesses there are processes that contain a series of steps performed by different people or different teams / departments. At each transition between the different groups is the potential for delay, error and misunderstanding. In our quest to reduce the lead time through becoming more effective we can take a simple look at our business, that of passing information (or products) through our business.

The relay race

When you take part in a relay race you can break down performance into two main elements. Firstly you need to be able to run fast. Secondly you need to be able to perform smooth handovers of the baton whilst still at speed.

If we take the simplistic view of our business as mentioned above then we are no different. We will specifically look at the running fast bit in a later section of the book. For now we will concentrate on the handovers as you don't win a race by dropping the baton!

Time lost

Each time a handover in the business is less than optimal we lose time. Most delays in a business are at these interfaces and by designing a better way to perform a handover we can improve how we perform for our customers. This does mean that we need to stop thinking as departments and start thinking as one business process.

Different departments have different ways of working and are often reluctant to change the way they work. In many cases if you start looking at the overall business and consider changes for 'the greater good' this battle lessens. You will still have a challenge on your hands but one you can overcome.

When discussing the handovers in your business get all of the necessary people together from the different teams and make sure people understand the issues at hand. Once they 'get it' and understand the need for these changes then the improvements should be easier to facilitate.

What could it be?

A lot of businesses find that their handovers fall into certain types, specific to their business. For some clients it is meetings that don't quite do the job (i.e. incomplete information passed between teams). For others it is in-trays, a stealth delay that can stretch out a job significantly. And one of the most common issues for poor handovers is inadequate decision making that takes place at the interface between the steps in the process.

Finding your type of handover problem can help you to find the other ones throughout the business process. Usually a pattern emerges once you identify your handover weaknesses.

Review your map

The logical next step is to review your map. Grouping the steps in the process into chunks – teams or departments for example – will help to see where the handovers take place.

Break down your business process so that you can see who all the key players are, whether this is individuals or departments.

Transaction issues

Facilitating a conversation between the two different groups is the next step (repeated for each 'transaction pair' on the chunked version of the map). This will need to be handled in a diplomatic fashion and will hopefully lead to some learning points around how to improve the handover.

Changes may include timing, format, missing information, too much information, personnel involved, standardisation etc.

Work through the discussion keeping in mind the principles for change determined at the start of this book. Which changes will help you to increase the value produced and help you achieve your brand?

Clarity of requirements

There may be many areas that will require further information. If this is the case then put the conversation on hold before proceeding. It is also a good idea to reflect upon the technical requirements of the handover as it is a good time to refresh the actual nature and necessity of the transaction. You may find that the transaction is no longer valid and can actually be removed (rather than improved).

So, the three things we are considering when discussing the handovers are:

- Do we still need this handover?

- Will an improvement to the handover improve our brand?

- Will an improvement to the handover increase our value adding capability?

Remove delays

One of the major noticeable benefits for improving handovers is removing delays. If you wanted to do a little research into your issues around handovers it would be worthwhile to find out how long it takes on average for work to be passed from one function into another before implementing the changes.

In some cases the delay will appear in the next process chunk if the handover is done in a push fashion. Work will build up at the next stage / department as a queue, and so whilst the handover would appear to be OK it is still affecting the next stage. It is worthy of review to see if a better handover would reduce the overall delay at the start of the next process.

For improvement purposes you might call the point where the work builds up at the handover step, a 'no man's land' so to speak. If there is clearly a clog in the system then this is the place to go to.

Improved team work

Another benefit from improving the handovers is that team working can improve between functions. When there is better understanding and a better flow of work between them life can become a little easier.

This isn't a magic wand approach, but making life easier for people is usually a great direction to move in!

Summary

Many lead time increasing delays can be found in the handovers between functions and departments. Identifying and streamlining these handovers is a great place to begin your improvement activities and can often bring very quick results to the business. As a bonus you may find that the working life of everyone involved improves just a little bit!

Action points

- Review your process map for the business and chunk it into groups based on departments / teams.

- Identify each handover step / action and find out what happens.

- Learn what should ideally happen at the handover to minimise delays, errors, frustrations etc. and re-design the activity.

- Look out for in-trays or piles of work building up just after the handover, and if necessary class this as part of the handover and get to work on it.

- Use this opportunity to improve the working relationships between functions in your business (or even your supply chain) by learning about each other and improving each other's working lives.

Example: Do it once, do it quickly

A construction based business was spending a large amount of time chasing their projects, missing deadlines and struggling to complete projects on time. One obvious issue was the link between the tendering and construction parts of the business. In terms of finding a handover of significance this was certainly a candidate.

As both departments were in the business a level of informality had appeared. The lack of formality meant that some communications didn't happen in the business and some bad practices had formed that a formal contractor would not accept, but that an internal customer would. Over time the needs of the construction department and the output from the tendering team diverged leading to a degree of rework taking place. The information being passed over wasn't suitable and the rework activity meant that projects started late, leading into the situation that we mentioned at the start of this example.

The formalities that were missing were reinstated (or defined for the first time in some areas) and proper, regimented, handover meetings were established. The information packs that were created by tendering were revised and this led to a smooth handover and an on time start of projects. The good practices then extended to other parts of the business, ultimately leading to a better project schedule adherence as further controls and handover improvements were made.

Improving your handovers can lead to better use of resources, increased productive capacity and higher levels of customer satisfaction. I hope you see from this example that looking at your handovers within your business is a worthwhile activity.

Sales Intake and Regulation

As good as your business becomes from the improved ways of working, you can still come unstuck if you fail to load your business with the right work at the right time, or are unable to flex your resources to match demand.

If you drive a diesel car then putting unleaded petrol into your fuel tank will cause a problem at some point in the near future. If you do not take work into your business in a manner appropriate for what you do then you may well find that similar problems occur. Like the cleaning of a car's fuel tank this problem will pass, but if we don't learn from our mistakes and keep on committing the same acts then eventually larger problems may arise. Put simply, if you fail to deliver your products and services due to poor capacity management then you may lose your customers' orders altogether.

This section of the book looks at using capacity tools and increasing certain aspects of business formality to properly receive work into the business, causing the minimum level of operational stress or disturbance possible.

Capacity models

When allowing work into the business it is essential to know what capacity you have available to deliver your products and services. This means that you need to know what your capacity limit is and what you have committed to already. By knowing these pieces of information you can easily schedule future pieces of work into your order book. This might sound like a really obvious point to make, but there are so many businesses who don't understand what they have available in terms of resources to deliver contracts that poor decisions are then made. You may have heard of these types of tools in the past, Rough Cut Capacity Planning and Master Production Scheduling (MPS) are two of the common terms used.

Although there can be a lot of science around capacity planning it is also possible to come up with a very basic approach that is approximately 95% accurate and allows you to manage your business effectively with little cost and negligible increases in administration time. The key is to understand what periods of time are appropriate to view in order to make decisions (days, weeks or months), how much of your current capacity has been committed in the chosen time period and what you have left to commit. If you have a business in which it is hard to aggregate your overall capacity into a single tool and you are unsure about how to proceed then a very simple approach could get you started. Identify your business' bottleneck and then develop the capacity plan around this one resource (process / machine / person). As you work to improve the throughput of this resource the bottleneck will move to the next place where throughput is restricted.

When this happens reconfigure your planning tool to the new bottleneck. This might sound fiddly, but it is a great problem to have as it tells you that your improvement activities are paying off. When you only schedule your bottleneck it means that you have the opportunity to flexibly use your other resources to deliver your products or services. Planning headaches can be minimised.

Contract review

Now that a robust capacity management tool is in place you will be able to arrange productive contract review meetings. The name of the meeting is not important, the purpose is that we create a more formal way for allowing work into our business. Depending on how your orders are received and how complex the work content is will determine the most appropriate method. Accepting orders without any form of consideration will leave you wide open to all kinds of knock on effects that can wreak some serious problems for your operations teams at a later date (and probably for the customer service team too!).

To determine your appropriate process is to determine what are all of the gates you need the order to pass through when it comes into the business and make sure that the relevant people, or information, is available when processing the order. For some businesses this takes the form of a quick meeting every day. For others this may appear as a web based tool, or a paper based checklist and a signature box.

If you need engineering input then there will need to be an engineering consideration.

If you need purchasing to confirm material availability then there will need to be a purchasing consideration.

If you need finance to confirm payment schedules then there will need to be a financial consideration.

You get the gist.

The simplest way to detail the contract review process is with a flow diagram, which can be used by an individual (or individuals in many separate locations) to accept an order and escalate to the appropriate department if issues occur. It can also be used as an agenda for a team to guide their thinking in a controlled and swift manner. My personal preference is to use a team approach as it stops pieces of paper (or e-mails) getting lost in people's filing systems and encourages speed. Once you get the hang of this process you will be able to run through the contract review very quickly.

Smoothing and scheduling

A massive benefit of running a contract review process is getting your workload scheduled at the right time with the right resources to ensure that you deliver with the least amount of strain on the business. This is one of the best situations to be in and helps you to deliver the best levels of customer service. Chaos can help to focus, but controlled and calm is an easier way to deliver a top class service.

To supplement your capacity planning tools it might be necessary from time to time to review the loading from a top level perspective. It might be that work has crept in, or delays on other work packages have caused some problems with the capacity plan. The schedule that has 'evolved' might push you past your capacity limits in certain areas and decisions will need to be taken in order to still satisfy the client in the most economical way.

Some options would include:

- Notifying the client and re-scheduling the work if possible.

- Using overtime or agency workers to provide a temporary capacity boost.

- Redeploying resources across the business if possible and returning them to their original roles once the 'bulge' in capacity has passed.

- Bringing work forwards if earlier weeks have available capacity.

Certain options are more suitable for different businesses and so coming up with your own selection is a good idea. By having your own selection of options the meetings to discuss any potential issues can run much more smoothly and quickly.

Summary

Take work into your business in a controlled manner that allows your business to work in the best way possible. Make sure that the filter / acceptance procedures that you create do just that. Use the information about the capacity of your business to make decisions and schedule the work accordingly. Don't overload your business, it causes breakdowns in the way people work and this risks disciplines being lost over time.

Action steps

- Create an acceptance procedure for your business and use this as a meeting agenda (or a checklist for an individual) when letting new orders into your business.

- Do not let any orders into your business without them passing the contract review stage.

- Develop simple capacity tools to allow you to schedule new orders entering your business.

- Periodically (weekly, for example) smooth and adjust your schedules based on the work already done and the work scheduled to start, so that your resources are optimised and that your customer gets what they want when they want it.

Example: Right time, right place

A manufacturing company was struggling to deliver their orders on time. Despite losing a handful of key staff the amount of work loaded into the business was higher than it had ever been. They were about to go into a holiday season too!

Subcontracting of work out of the business was also at a new all time high and so far they had paid lip service to their Master Production Scheduling tools (MPS). I suggested that they started to be more controlled about how they allocated their capacity when work came into the business through a contract review meeting.

"It will take hours" I was told. My response was that this would be one of the best uses of their time and that after a few days of getting used to the meeting that it would only take minutes. The first day it took nearly three hours and not much quicker over the next three or four days. Thankfully they got the hang of it, realised its importance and got the meeting down to around ten minutes.

Just by putting the right work in the right slots their on-time delivery performance shot up, and their lead times came down as well as their capacity actually increasing (due to a reduction in fire fighting / chasing late orders).

Overtime also reduced and subcontracting needs diminished too, all with a greater overall output each and every month.

All of this was a result from 'just' putting one daily meeting in place.

Discipline and Routines

Cause and effect

Now that we have come this far I hope you are happy with the idea of cause and effect. There will be certain tasks that take place within your business that will help your business to perform and achieve its objectives. Knowing what these are and ensuring that they take place is what this section is all about.

Review the map

The first task in this section is to review the process map and identify all of the points on the map that make a difference to the product or service being delivered. There will be a handful of items that pop out immediately that are just like this. Get your list together and then use the phrase 'so that' to link them up into a logical sequence of events. This test will help to make sure that you have identified them all.

For example,

- We allow work into our business when we have available capacity SO THAT

- We order our materials in order to start production on time SO THAT

- We can deploy the right resources to the right job SO THAT

- We despatch the orders on time SO THAT

- We invoice as quickly as possible SO THAT

- We retain our clients and maximise our profits.

Key tasks

There will be many tasks that occur every day; the idea behind this section is that we identify the handful of important daily tasks that keep the whole process going. Some are critical and need to be up to date every single day (or more frequently depending in their purpose), but some aren't. It is up to you to make a distinction. When you have a handful of key tasks you are ready to move on.

What doesn't happen?

Once you have compiled a list of key tasks you may also want to create a list of things that just don't get done. In most cases these small tasks build up and eventually cause one part of the system to fall over, resulting in fire fighting activities. Creating routines is a great way to improve the levels of discipline in the business and including supporting areas of the business system is a great opportunity.

Create a schedule – the business timetable

Now that these lists have been created we can create a schedule for the business. You may well have some kind of time table already in place, if you do then this is an opportunity to review, refine and expand as appropriate. Having one timetable for the whole business keeps everything running in sync. One department knows when to complete various parts of its workload in order for another part to be able to deliver its products or services.

Many businesses work brilliantly using time tables.

Schools and buses spring to mind, the approach works and it can work for your business too. When functions within a business don't know when to complete their tasks (especially routine tasks) then performance suffers. The time tables can be simple and you may want them to reach over different time periods. There may be daily, weekly, monthly and yearly activities to consider.

Personal timetables

For certain members of staff a personal timetable might be appropriate. People who have multiple responsibilities can benefit from this approach if they have a problem with managing their time and delivering their results. If you do go down this avenue please work with the person / people in question as it can make their day become more rigid and getting their buy in will help enormously.

I've seen this approach generate great results, if the person has a problem with delivering their services at the right time to the right standard - if they are willing to have this conversation. A milder version of this is to give them a checklist for the day / week and as long as all of the tasks are complete each day / week (depending on their requirement) then this gives the person a priority system (and is a little more palatable for most people).

Regulation

Keeping all of these tasks in check and making sure that everything is happening is essential, the next section of this book covers this topic in more depth.

Summary

Create a list of the tasks that need to happen like clockwork and create time tables for your business. Building upon these timetables and making the tasks into habits will develop disciplines in your business which can bring with them a whole raft of other benefits. The idea of the time table is not to make your business rigid, but to ensure that the right work gets done at the right time, but to leave you with enough gaps in your diary so that flexibility is maintained. Getting the right balance between routine and flexibility is the goal of this section.

Action steps

- Review your map and identify the key tasks that are 'at cause' that need to happen like clockwork.

- Create a time table for your business that everyone agrees to.

- Work with individuals to create checklists or personal time tables as appropriate to overcome (internal) delivery problems.

- Link this work with the section on 'regulation'.

Example: Fish on Friday

One of my earlier clients was failing to implement the changes and habits necessary to make the difference to the performance of the operation of their business. They told me that they wanted to make the changes, but they struggled to cope with the amount of things that they needed to do and that their 'day to day' got in the way.

It's a common story, and we solved their particular problem through a story about this particular person's mother!

When I asked my client if they could tell me about anyone who was disciplined and followed a routine they started to tell me about their mum, and how she would cook fish every Friday without fail (they were devout Catholics in case you were wondering).

So, we created 'fish on Friday'. Its first incarnation was a rota of activities and effectively served as a timetable to keep the key activities on track. It might sound too simple, but it works. When the chaos is all around you then something simple to get you back on track is all it takes.

My client has developed it since then, but the fundamental principle is still in place. We defined what was important for everyone in the team, when it needed to be done by and then made sure that it was one of the first jobs of the day.

Regulation of Resources

The way that your business regulates its resources can have a big impact on how effective it is at giving the customer what they want, when they want it. This section looks at some simple ideas on how to build regulation into the working day.

Review the map

If you look back over the map you created for your business you will see that there are points within the process that are critical. There are behaviours that are also critical and these affect your performance directly. For every point, whether it is a handover, a measurement, a checklist, a computer program, an action or an approval gate, getting people together to evaluate quickly the overall picture and then re-deploy resources can make a big impact on the way that your business performs. Many of the points we are talking about will have been defined in the 'run like clockwork' section.

Killer questions

For each point that is of importance it may be helpful

to define what I would call a 'killer question', one that can be asked in quick team meetings that help to regulate business activities. The question is designed to get right to the core of what is meant to happen for the business in a way that a 'yes' or a 'no' are the only suitable answers. The reason for getting down to such a simple response is that it can speed up a meeting enormously. The last thing that I would want for your business is to get bogged down in unproductive meetings!

If we took the example of a person who was responsible for the quotations in the business we could ask "have all of the due quotations been sent out to our customers?" If the answer is 'yes', that's great (and no doubt the quality of our quotations will be linked to our win rate, which we would measure elsewhere). If the answer is 'no' then a quick update of "when will you catch up?" should be sufficient.

Any unacceptable answers of course may be followed up outside of a meeting environment for the purpose of reducing the overall time for people to spend in meetings (as the other seven people who aren't in your two person conversation at this point don't need to be present).

If we looked at the example of a sales manager who was responsible for keeping our order books loaded fully for 'x' months ahead we could ask "are the order books loaded at 100% for the next x months?" Again, a 'no' response could be followed up with a standard question of "when will this be achieved?" with any longer dialogue being taken outside of the main meeting.

Sunrise meetings

To pull the various questions together it is usually helpful to have a quick team meeting of some sort to run through the 'killer questions' and to ensure that direction for the team is appropriate to the day's upcoming challenges. Depending on how your business operates this could be first thing in the working day (a sunrise meeting), just before the end (a sunset meeting), or at any time that suits the way that you work. The idea is that the key people meet to discuss the key points every day and make sure that everything is on track.

A fixed agenda for the meeting made up primarily from the killer questions is all you need. To keep the pace of the meeting quick it is usually worthwhile defining a time limit for the meeting, this helps to manage expectations / diaries and keeps the process as slick as possible. It is very easy for a daily meeting of this nature to get distracted by the (necessary) discussions around the business' problems which can eventually take over the original format. This meeting is a swift check of what has happened and what needs to happen. Anything outside of this agenda needs to be addressed outside of the meeting. Simple.

S&OP

One of the tools developed decades ago that has stood the test of time is the 'Sales and Operations Planning' process. Unfortunately many newer businesses haven't been subjected to this approach and are missing out on a simple way to regulate activities in various parts of the business. Although there are many excellent books on the subject it does seem to lend itself to a manufacturing enterprise more easily than any other kind. That is until you strip out the principles and apply them generally.

The crux of the process is to gather the people responsible for each business function and then determine whether their function is on track, behind or ahead with regards to their contribution to the business plan. If they are behind they need help, if they are ahead they may need to slow down and if they are on track - great job. It could be argued that if all functions are ahead of schedule then that is a brilliant situation to have, and I agree.

Usually, however, it is the case that one function is way ahead, most are on track and a couple are lagging behind. In this scenario it is usually more desirable to move resources from the function doing well to help those that are lagging behind, for the common good of the business.

I must also state here that S&OP also involves an update and a forecast of activities in each area. This additional information is there to help make a decision on how far behind, ahead or otherwise a function is. For example, the R&D team may be ahead of schedule and the Finance team far behind, but if the Marketing function declare that they are on the brink of winning a whole load of new contracts that require heavy R&D support you may not choose to help out the Finance team by redeploying resources (i.e. from within the R&D team) due to the new information.

Regulation, agility and plan 'B'

It might sound all well and good moving resources from one function to another, but often there is a skill / training issue in doing so. Often multi-skilling is the domain of the shop floor or the construction site, but this approach is also applicable in office based functions of the business. If you're struggling to visualise this then consider the game of rugby. When the ball goes off the side of the pitch and a line out is called everyone knows where they need to be and what they need to do. There is no consultation or negotiation, the resources are reconfigured until the situation passes and then everyone returns to what they were doing in order to execute the original strategy.

The Plan 'B' that I refer to in the heading is a clear understanding of what your resources need to do when the situation changes significantly. The sorts of things I am referring to include: loss of a big customer, recession, quality problems affecting multiple customers etc.. If you are unconvinced - do your staff know what to do in the event of a fire? Once the fire has passed, it's usually back to normal. This is how your business could operate should a significant change in the working environment occurs.

Summary

By understanding what the critical points in your process are you can quickly define a handful of 'killer questions' that can form the agenda for a very short operational meeting. The responses to these questions can then allow adjustments to be made in terms of what help is required and in which part of the business (although some training may be required for this to become a reality).

Use of the S&OP and plan 'B' approaches can help a business to become more flexible and in tune with the moving pressures within the business, again allowing for flexibility in delivering the production plan / business plan.

Action points

- Identify the critical points in the process.

- Create 'killer questions'.

- Implement a daily (Sunrise) meeting and help all functions to help each other.

- Implement a monthly S&OP type meeting where the progress of each function is considered against the business plan, and adjust activity accordingly.

- Create a few scenarios that could happen to your

business and define how (and who) the business would need to operate should the scenario occur.

Example: Getting the right answer

One of my clients was struggling to understand how their business was doing going forwards. Their Sales Director always spoke about the sales pipeline and it always sounded good. The problem was that with such a good pipeline the order books and turnover didn't catch up.

When I talked with the Managing Director later on in the working day I asked him what he really wanted to know. He had become befuddled by the Sales Director and so I suggested to him that he may want to know "do we have a full order book for the next three months?"

I was then informed that I was being soft and that it should be six months ahead!

The point was made and the change was clear. Every week from then on the question was a lot more explicit and a 'yes' or 'no' was elicited. There was no wiggle room and when the answer was 'no' then it was a subject for a later conversation. Corrections were made, plans were executed and sales volumes increased.

The Managing Director naturally applied the same thinking to the rest of his senior team, and from the increased focus came higher levels of productivity and profit.

Improving Your Processes

So far all of the things we have covered in this book are aimed at improving the effectiveness of your business processes. This section finally considers ideas to help you become more efficient in your business by looking at making the processes you use as good as they can be.

Review your map

You map will most likely be made up of a collection of steps or sub-processes. A process is something that converts something into something else, so defining the processes that take place in your business won't be too difficult if you have your map. The map has been focussed on your order conversion process but the following approaches can be applied outside of these areas. Other processes within your business will benefit from this section just as much as your order delivery system. A system, by the way, is a collection of processes that work together to deliver a result. For simplicity in this section we are going to be looking at the individual processes as a start to finish entity in their own rights.

Segmentation / prioritisation

The first thing to do with our map then is to break it down into discreet processes, to define their scopes. Some processes might cover a handful of steps on your map, or be a single step. It is important that you are clear on what these processes are.

For each process we need to know the point at which it starts and the point at which it ends. The triggers for the start or end points may be tangible or intangible outputs or inputs. Defining these points as richly as possible is essential before we continue.

There is also a decision to be made about where to start with the process improvement work. By this I am referring to the priorities you need to make to ensure that you get the best use of your time. You will probably have a gut instinct about where to start, it will be the process that causes the most problems, has the poorest yield, is the bottle neck etc. If in doubt get some facts and figures (as well as some opinion) to make a decision on the priorities.

List your processes and prioritise.

Improvement team members

The next consideration is the people who are going to

be involved with the improvement. Ideally you will get the people who are responsible and involved with the process to take part. You will need people who have direct intimate knowledge of the process to provide information. You will also benefit from including some people who aren't familiar to ask the so called 'daft questions' that can sometimes lead to a breakthrough. Please don't rely on just people from the second group though!

Prior to any work being started it is good to get the team together to explain the overall objectives you have and the work that is going to take place. You may need to do some training with the team as ideally you will give each person a task during the process analysis stage. The key tools are detailed below.

Process flow analysis + other tools

The tools listed below are simple and effective. There are more tools, but the tools we are looking at here are a great collection that can be picked up at short notice and used to great effect. All of the tools listed below are to be used at the same time during the data gathering activity.

PFA - Process Flow Analysis

This core tool allows us to track the work as it moves through its process. These processes are often referred to as value streams as we are keen on minimising the amount of time the work spends in the process, so that the value adding elements are maximised. This worksheet can be found at the end of this section.

Each step of our process is to be recorded on this sheet. We are going to record any distance travelled and the time taken for that step. We are also going to classify the step as either:

- An operation - we do something.

- A delay - the next step has to wait for someone / something.

- A transport - we need to physically move something.

- An inspection - we need to stop and review.

- A storage - we put something into storage.

Any additional notes can also be made against each step. For the time and distance measures try to keep your units consistent throughout the recordings (e.g. metres and minutes).

Spaghetti Map

This next tool is great for the artist of the group! This

tool tracks the physical location of the work on a map of some kind. If you have a pre-drawn map of a working area then that is ideal, otherwise a sketch of the work area will need to be made prior to starting the data gathering. The steps to complete the map are as follows:

- Draw a sketch of the area.

- Plot the starting location of the work.

- Follow each step of the process by drawing the route that the work takes.

- Label each point on the map with the corresponding number from the Process Flow Analysis sheet.

- Continue until the process has been mapped out completely.

Wastes

Whilst working your way through the process you will undoubtedly find steps that make you wonder if that is the best way to do the work. In addition to your questioning skills is a very useful tool that helps to categorise work, it is known as 'the seven wastes'.

The Seven Wastes are:

- Defects - doing something incorrectly.

- Overproduction - doing too much of something.

- Transport - moving things unnecessarily.

- Waiting - putting up with delays

- Inventory - holding too much 'stock'.

- Motions - using too much human effort to complete the work.

- Processes - not having the best way of working.

There is also another waste (entitled 'the eighth waste') which looks at untapped human potential, meaning that the people involved with the job are not being allowed to use their ideas to make things better. As each step of the process is reviewed we can work out if these steps are in fact waste and if so what type of waste it is. This tool can help make the obscure obvious. Again, each step can be labelled up to correspond with the process flow analysis.

A copy of a waste recording sheet can be found at the end of this section.

Notes / observations

To accompany the other forms of recording it is also handy to have another member of the team record their observations, thoughts and questions about the process that they are observing. These additional notes and insights can aid the next step in the analysis of the process.

A blank sheet of paper, a pen and a curious (attentive) mind are all that is required.

Review / concern-cause-countermeasure

Once you have recorded the steps of the process there are two things we need to do before we create our plan.

The first step is to work out how much time has been spent in the process, and how much time has been spent on value adding steps. The ideal situation is to have both numbers the same. So, get your calculator out and work out what these two numbers are. They will give you direction for your improvement. You may choose to refine your analysis so that you can identify pockets of non-value adding time, the tasks that are candidates for immediate eradication.

The second thing to do is to be clear about what concerns you have about the process. The sheet at the end of this section can be used to help format your team's thoughts. Every step in the process that isn't to your liking can be recorded as a concern. Each part that isn't adding value to your customer in the most straightforward and simple way could be a concern. Don't worry about how many your team add to the list, just list them.

Next to each concern should be a cause - why does this concern exist. If the answer isn't obvious then drill down past the symptoms until you reach something fundamental. If you are unsure about doing this then refer to '5 WHY' in the second section of this book. Once you know the root cause the countermeasure usually becomes obvious.

For each concern (now with its identified cause) you need to determine a suitable countermeasure so that the concern disappears. When you have done this then you are ready for the plan of attack.

PDCA tracking

PDCA stands for:

- PLAN – define your goal and your plan.

- DO – execute your plan.

- CHECK – review your results.

- ACT – decide what to do next.

>- Tweak the plan and try again.

>- Document the change and move on to another opportunity.

Not all improvements turn out the way we want them to the first time round. The PDCA process is also known as the 'continuous improvement cycle' and should be seen as a cycle.

Using this approach to track your improvement projects reminds us of two things: Firstly, if we don't get the result we want then we need to try again; and secondly, if the change has worked then we need to record the change somehow so we don't forget what we have done (and slip back into old ways).

An example format for this tracking sheet is at the end of this section. More details on PDCA can be found in a later chapter.

Make changes

Now you have a list it is time to get moving and make the improvements happen. Motivation at the start of a change project can either be difficult (because we have seen it all before) or easy (finally we get to make some changes). The key to sustaining change is to support the people making projects a consistent and regular event. Once a week is a good place to start to have a short (and I mean short – 15 minutes or so) catch up on where we are with the (mini) projects.

Failure to support the ongoing work is how these kinds of projects fail – so whatever you do – don't stop meeting up, talking and supporting. People can lose the faith easily and you need to prove them wrong by seeing this through. Remember if you are in doubt – go for smaller chunks (we'll talk more about this later on in the book).

Learning and recording

The worst thing that can happen when you make the

improvements identified above is that the benefits might not materialise immediately. You might not achieve the results immediately and therefore this becomes an opportunity for learning.

Every change you make will give you a new insight as to how things work in your business. Capture these insights and build them up into your own guide for further improvement. When you do get some new knowledge this is a brilliant opportunity to make the next attempt even more likely to work, or be even better than you originally anticipated.

Schedule the 're-match'

When you have been through this process and have improved how discrete parts of your business operate, then it is time to put a date in the diary to do it all again. As I said above, the information that you get from doing it differently will make you a different person and when you approach process improvement again you will see the business differently.

Repeating this process is one of the keys to making the improvements significant and aids the stickability of the changes. After a while this will become 'the way we do it round here'. Change can be the standard.

Is this slick?

A great question to ask yourself about each of your processes is 'is this slick?'.

If you can't say 'yes' to this question then you might want to have another go at it straight away. When you are happy with what you have done then put the next review date in your diary and move on to the next pressing issue (from a process improvement point of view at least!).

Summary

There are a variety of simple steps and tools available to help you rapidly and radically improve how discrete parts of your business work. It is also a great way to get different members of the business to work together for the common good. Their different perspectives and skills make this process a far more interesting, creative and effective process. Use the worksheets at the end of this section to run your own improvement sessions and see what improvements you can make.

Action steps

- Chunk your processes from your map of the business processes and prioritise what needs doing.

- Get a team together who have different points of views / skills.

- Walk through a process using the worksheets and observe and question – but don't judge yet.

- Collate all of the findings and then judge.

- Find out the root causes of the concerns and create solutions to truly remedy the concerns.

- Chip away at the improvements, a little every week is better than a big blowout followed by nothing at all.

- Keep going until the process is 'slick'.

- Choose a date for the next session of improvement for this process.

- Move to the next process that you have prioritised.

Process				Date			Sheet /
No	Step (Description)	Time	Dist	Activity Type[1]	VA[2]	Comments / Notes	
				O ⇒ ▷ D ☐			
				O ⇒ ▷ D ☐			
				O ⇒ ▷ D ☐			
				O ⇒ ▷ D ☐			
				O ⇒ ▷ D ☐			
				O ⇒ ▷ D ☐			
				O ⇒ ▷ D ☐			
				O ⇒ ▷ D ☐			
				O ⇒ ▷ D ☐			
				O ⇒ ▷ D ☐			

[1] O Operation, ⇒ Transport, ▽ Storage, D Delay, ☐ Inspection | [2] VA = Value Adding Step (Yes / No)

Waste Walk Sheet

Name of Process: _____

Date of walk: _____

Waste Identified	Where?
Defects	
Overproduction	
Transport	
Waiting	
Inventory	
Motions	
Processes	
Untapped Human Potential	

Date:		
Process:		Sheet /

Concern	Cause	Countermeasure

PDCA Tracking Format

Date	Area / Project	Concern	Action (P)	Responsible	Due (D)	Actual Complete	Check Results (C)	Next Step (A)	Notes

Example: How quick?

One of the businesses I worked in as an engineer was suffering from growing lead times. We had increased the variety of our product range and this increased complexity had led to a number of problems that manifested them as taking longer and longer to get the job done.

From watching how the work was done it was clear that the problem was in two areas, the layout and some element of communication.

Using the tools we have talked about in this section we changed how the products flowed through the business. We also used our Enterprise Resources Planning (ERP) system to coordinate more effectively with our Stores department to get the kits pulled together at the right time.

After a lot of heartache we got the changes put in place and we found that our lead time came down from nearly twenty weeks to under ten.

We then also used one of the ideas from an earlier section of this book and adjusted how we accepted work into the business. The reduced confusion took our lead time down to under four weeks and we became one of the fastest companies in our industry, which led to more orders for the business.

Definitely a positive result all round!

Part 2 - Fuel for the Engine

Continuous Improvement Matrix
Focus on a small part of the business and ideas flow.

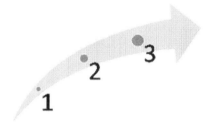

Kaizen
Use tiny steps to gain momentum, motivation and confidence.

PDCA
Come up with a good idea and then iterate it until it works.

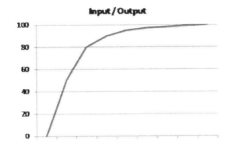

80/20
Some improvement activities will help a lot, some won't.

Find Root Causes
Keep digging until you find the real issues.

Simplify Job Roles
Gist and purpose can improve clarity and effectiveness.

Effective Continuous Improvement

Continuous Improvement (CI) is a well used term. Most businesses seem to love the idea of CI but struggle with implementing it. Whilst a lot of people see CI as the final area of change within a Lean programme it can be a great way to kick start a business into making changes. CI, however, should be more of a way of life for a business rather than some big event or promotion.

Bad to OK

Many businesses that I have encountered have already put in place some form of continuous improvement activity. Many of them generate improvements rapidly but often falter for one of two main reasons. Firstly, there is no follow up to the change idea - it doesn't get implemented. Secondly, the CI work only focuses on fixing problems, they don't look at making things wildly better.

OK to brilliant

When you have a problem to resolve your focus is easy. Moving from OK to brilliant is hard, after all if I can see a problem I can come up with some ideas to get it back to its normal operating state. This is moving us from bad to OK. When the problem isn't clear it can be far harder.

There is no definition of how good a process or function can be, and therefore we can get lost with the size of the challenge. Keep striving to be better and see where the journey takes you.

Tiny insights

When we break the improvement opportunities down into tiny bite sized chunks we will see that improvements flow from all different levels within the business.

To get CI moving from OK to Brilliant we can therefore stimulate this action by artificially creating tiny chunks to consider.

Improvement matrix

To create tiny chunks one of the options we can use is to create an improvement matrix.

This simple tool has tasks / processes / functions along the top and improvement considerations down the side (such as 'faster', 'cheaper', 'prettier' etc.). This produces a grid - the improvement matrix, as demonstrated overleaf.

	Task 1	Task 2	Task 3	Task 4
Factor 1				
Factor 2				
Factor 3				
Factor 4				
Factor 5				

Routine meeting

To use this matrix you will need a team of people from across the business, and at all different levels. We recommend meeting once per week, although you can increase the frequency to suit the urgency of your requirements. Less than fortnightly is not recommended as momentum can be lost.

The agenda for the meeting could be (please amend as you improve it!):

- Review previous agreed actions [not relevant to first meeting].

- Choose one area from the grid that hasn't been reviewed yet.

- Brainstorm ideas (no judgements) about how to do Task X in order to improve by Factor Y.

- Choose best idea, assign task and deadline (usually next meeting is ideal) and record the information centrally.

- Update the box on the grid with today's meeting.

- Confirm date and time of next meeting.

Ideally the meetings will be short and effective, perhaps no longer than 15 minutes. The initial meeting might take much longer as your team finds its feet.

Each time work on another grid box until they all have dates in them. Once you have a 'full house' you can start again. Reviewing the factors and the tasks is worth doing every rotation as priorities can change due to new knowledge and understanding from the changes you have already made.

Expansion of the CI process

This whole process can be packaged for individual work areas across the business and multi-disciplinary teams can be used to develop and implement the ideas as described above. You will need to find what split works best for you, as you may have too many processes or tasks to fit onto one grid.

Summary

Continuous Improvement activities often fail when we move away from being bad at something and become OK. Use tiny focal points to create an abundance of improvement ideas that can move your business forwards.

Action points

- Split your business down into tasks / processes.

- Define how your business could improve - "factors".

- Create the continuous improvement matrix.

- Get a team together and use the described agenda to start generating ideas.

- Implement the ideas, complete the matrix and then repeat.

Example: The office junior is the star

A client who was doing well knew there were things to improve but just couldn't put their finger on what to do. It was just a feeling, but nothing was broken so to speak.

Using a matrix like the one in this section we got the team together and defined the factors and tasks. As soon as we defined the matrix we had our first meeting.

To prove that it was useable by all I invited the most junior member of staff to pick an area on the grid. Without prompting this member of staff who had only been with the company for two weeks, and who was fairly quiet, started a monologue of all the things you could do to improve that particular combination.

Slightly flabbergasted the Managing Director got out her pad of paper and started to try and capture the ideas that this member of staff was generating.

This particular story could have been told on any week that this tool was used. Their new problem was how to implement the ideas that were being generated because there were so many!

Getting Things Moving

When we have so many opportunities to improve, it can often be frustrating to find that nothing is actually progressing. The day to day work can get in the way for sure, but no progress at all?

Keep talking

Projects and tasks that stall are very common in business improvement. It's one thing to identify an improvement and come up with a plan. It's a very different thing when it comes to making the changes happen. If you are finding this happen in your business then it is critical that you keep the dialogue going, that you find a way to discuss these issues and find ways to help your team make progress.

Deadlines are a good way to maintain clarity with others. This requires you of course to intervene and make a decision as to what is important and when you want it completed by. Artificial deadlines can work, but ideally we want the motivation to come from the individual.

Fight or flight - the modern problem

When a task looks overwhelming and a person cannot get their head around how they can complete the necessary activity they are likely to procrastinate and put the task on hold. This is the fight or flight response in action; in this example they are in flight and have run away from the issue (in their heads at least). Thankfully the solution to overcome this issue of delay is quite simple.

The size of a task can be a subjective issue. What is large to one person is insignificant to another. Usually the only size people can agree upon is what is tiny. When I refer to tiny here we have to search for the smallest unit possible. A tiny step or action usually does not stimulate the fight or flight response and allows progress to be made.

Tiny steps

Tiny in our case is ridiculously tiny. So tiny that it seems a waste of time even contemplating. When you have shrunk down the first step so that it seems trivial you will be on the right lines.

There is often a lot of resistance to making the first steps absolutely tiny because the goal then seems so far away. This first step is about ignition - getting the project started up and should have little reflection upon the rest of the project, although some ramp up may be required.

Momentum

When people can get a couple of small steps completed their motivation and confidence raises, allowing them to tackle bigger and more difficult steps. When they come up with a way to complete their day to day tasks and still make improvements they will be in a great place. As they make improvements to the way they work as well as the way the business operates more time is freed up - to help them accept more workload, or to make even more improvements to the business.

As the steps become bigger your workforce will be more capable and willing to make changes within the business. The results of becoming a better business can be reinforced with your customers and if marketed correctly can lead to winning more business.

Innovation

When enough confidence and experience has been gained you can find that the area of innovation can be visited more easily. Making a leap within a business can be a scary thing, but when people have experience of change, and of constantly changing environments, then performing work in a completely different manner seems more possible.

The changes we have discussed through this book are based on improvement, doing what we do better. Innovation can completely change the approach leading to larger gains more quickly, but this comes with higher risks in many cases. Having the tools of continuous improvement are important for the times when innovation ideas aren't readily available. There is also the issue that, because of the upheaval innovation can cause, you need to schedule it and be controlled with it. With continuous improvement you can drip feed the changes and become a better performing business almost by stealth. One day you will look back and see how far you have come. Having both Continuous Improvement and Innovation in your toolkit is essential.

Summary

If projects are stalling then finding a new way forward is required if progress is to be maintained. Taking advantage of what we know about fight or flight is a great way to do just this. Break down your early project tasks into tiny packets of work, so tiny that they seem ridiculous. Let people find their own confidence and momentum and then sit back and watch as progress is made.

Action points

- Find a way to keep an ongoing conversation about the improvements that need to take place. A weekly meeting, a daily chat - whatever works for you and your team.

- Find stalled projects and break the first few steps (until the first milestone?) into tiny steps.

- If you come up against any form of inertia then consider tiny steps the whole way. At least the project will conclude - better at a slower pace than not at all.

Example: The massive pile of invoices

The technique of 'tiny steps' has appeared so many times in my projects over the years that it is sometimes hard to choose the most prominent story. But here goes.

One client had failed to deal with their invoicing for a number of months. Cash flow was suffering and the Office Manager was getting distressed at the amount of paperwork building up. The Managing Director had to OK the invoices and didn't like being in the office. Before I arrived in the business they had already decided that the answer was for the Managing Director to spend every Wednesday in the office. He hated being in the office.

So, the work never got done.

I negotiated that the Managing Director would spend the first ten minutes of the day working with the Office Manager, but that only five minutes could be spent on invoicing issues. I was told that this would not work, but they agreed that it was better than nothing.

Unsurprisingly, within one week most of the invoicing was dealt with. The Managing Director realised that it didn't take long to sort out the mess when it was provided to him in small packets. And, as with most kaizen / tiny steps type interventions, he started to do more than we had originally requested.

This short meeting was then used to leverage in other

improvements that they needed, but had previously felt that they didn't have time for.

Tiny steps win again!

Experiment and Make Progress

Many improvements don't get implemented. Many ideas to make the business work better never see the light of day. Many attempts are half hearted when we try to change what we do and we happily cancel the improvements before they get too serious.

There is so much pressure on getting things right at work that the one area of business where experimentation and 'trial and error' plays a useful part gets repressed. The result is that we don't bother any more, improvements stop happening naturally. There is a remedy for this and thankfully it is very simple.

PDCA

You have probably come across the PDCA, or 'Plan Do Check Act', cycle before. We touched upon it earlier in this book. It is a very simple tool that many people choose to ignore. It is at the core of many business improvement processes and it's the same process that a baby goes through when they are learning to walk. In summary PDCA is about not giving up when your ideas don't work, it is about trying a different approach until you get your desired result. The four steps to PDCA are:

Plan - Come up with a game plan to achieve your objective (improvement target).

Do - Execute the plan.

Check - Review how well you achieved your result.

Act - Decide on what you are going to do next. Try again with a few modifications to your approach, or close down the activity and crystallise the information somewhere within the business.

The usual stopping point

Many people leap straight into the Do part of the cycle. Their Plan is not always in their head (let alone on paper), and they head straight for execution. This is the usual response. If you work in a high pressure environment then taking the time to think through your options (remember the 80 / 20 rule? See the next section if not) seems like a luxury when in most cases it actually saves you time.

When the action fails to yield the necessary improvement it is often seen as not being worthwhile to continue and the activity is wound down before being forgotten about. The improvement activity ceases.

Worse still, the pressure that caused the need for change (usually externally motivated rather than coming from a team focussed on discovery and interest in the process) may have been removed when progress is seen by the person applying the pressure. A little progress and the person disappears! When the problem resurfaces then this whole situation will repeat itself.

The Check phase in this PDCA tool is not about comparing

where you are with where you want to be. It is even more subjective than 'working' or 'not working'. There is always a grey area and we need to ask ourselves if the improvement could be 'better' if we approached it differently next time. The Check and Act stages are neglected in many businesses, the right questions are not asked and improvements stall.

If we take a little bit of time to come up with an effective Plan, Do the execution required, Check to see if we got the results we needed and then Act upon these findings we can help our improvements along nicely.

The baby doesn't give up after 'x' attempts at walking, they iterate their approach, learn from their mistakes and suddenly (as it appears to us!) one day they start walking. All of the effort, attempts and frustrations are accepted because the result is worth having. PDCA.

Blend PDCA and kaizen

A useful modification to the PDCA approach is to blend it with the Kaizen idea of tiny steps. A barrier that is often cited for not making changes is the fear of the improvement going wrong and causing knock on problems for the business. If this is the case then we can use PDCA on a tiny improvement (or pilot project) and then use each successive cycle to grow the improvement's scope until it is ready for roll out.

Taking the fear and concern of management away from the improvement process is invaluable. Making changes and improvements in a subtle manner can make life so much easier.

Sometimes you cannot afford this luxury, but in many cases you can. If you are struggling to try out new things then blend the two approaches together.

Close out

One of the saddest things you can watch is a business re-discovering their improvements. The phrase 'we tried that years ago, and it didn't work!' means that we failed to work out a way for that idea to work.

The phrase 'we used to do that years ago' closely follows the previous statement and means that we failed to capture the good ideas and good practices and allowed time to pass to the point that we forgot what we should be doing.

When you get a successful change taking place it is key to work out what to do with the new information. Some of the things you can do include creating new instructions on how to run parts of the business, writing a memo, holding a meeting, changing your training approach, or something else. Don't let the new information / insights / discoveries disappear – lock them into the business in whatever way is appropriate.

Tracking progress

PDCA is a great way to manage business improvement tasks. When you get a plethora of improvements from looking at a particular issue within your business it is easy to lose the ideas from half hearted improvements. When you consider the effectiveness of the improvement (Check stage) and close out improvements effectively (Act stage) you can achieve a far higher rate of improvement than just having a big list of improvements to tick off a list.

Reflecting upon the Plan stage of PDCA also suggests that we spend a little bit more time thinking about how we are going to tackle the improvement. Getting off to the right start obviously makes a difference, and knowing that PDCA is a simple yet effective tool to support improvement means that we can take a little more time over our changes. A steady progressive stroll towards being a better business is usually preferable to a panicked rush to try and change everything.

Summary

PDCA (Plan Do Check Act) is a tool that everyone can understand and use, but rarely do we see it consistently applied in the work place. When we use the approach to properly close out improvements we find that our changes are far more sustainable. When we crystallise the learning in the business we are able to progress faster and consistently in the right (and only) direction. Ideas that we generate don't get lost, we try them out properly and keep working at them until they work and they make a real difference to the business. When we get swamped with ideas for improvement we can use PDCA with our other tools to properly manage them through to completion. Improvement is no longer guesswork as to where we are up to and what works, we become systematic and thorough.

Action points

- Share the PDCA tool with your team.

- Apply PDCA to all of your business improvement activities.

- Create an improvement tracking spreadsheet that incorporates the elements of Plan Do Check Act, in a way that makes sense to you.

Example: Making it safe for management

One of my clients struggled to make changes happen within their business. Their management team had suffered the backlash of failure from trying new things in the past and not succeeding in getting them to work. They were now risk averse, but they knew that they needed to change and so I was called in to help them.

As mentioned in the previous section, we used a combination of tiny steps (kaizen) and the PDCA process to offer them a way of dipping their toes into the improvements, without the risk of failure associated with their previous large improvement initiatives that had failed.

Each improvement that we developed was split up into stages of maturity. These stages included a tiny initial trial phase, expansion and roll out. Some projects were able to be split up more and would have a different number of stages. The principle however was that we would offer improvements that had a progression plan. Start small (and low risk) and then using the continuous improvement cycle grow and develop the improvement into its full potential.

Using the PDCA tool allowed this client to control their improvements, and when combined with a progression plan they were able to feel a lot more comfortable about how they approached improvement generally.

Prioritisation

Time is not an infinite resource in the work place. We only have so many hours per day that we have available or are willing to use. One consideration we should make is that we need to decide which improvement projects are going to be worth following up on and which ones can be put on the back burner.

The flow of ideas

When you have your continuous improvement activities taking place on a regular basis you will likely be faced with a large number of actions or paths that you can take. Some will take you on a path of high performance and some will take you a lot of effort for relatively poor returns. This is quite normal, in this case however we want to put some thinking into our choices before we proceed.

Pareto principle

If you have come across the Pareto principle, also known as the 80/20 rule, you will understand precisely this dilemma. Some projects will give you a massive return on your efforts, whilst most projects will give you a poor return on your efforts. Referring to the 80/20 notation - 80% of your results will come from 20% of your projects.

This peculiar economics principle urges us to be selective with our projects.

Choosing what to follow up

Measuring the outputs based on Pareto thinking can be difficult. We can however come up with a set of decision principles that we can use to make this assessment easier.

With your team come up with a handful of requirements around your ideal improvement. You can include elements from your brand also at this point.

For example, the following list may be selected:

- Improves our appearance with our customers

- Is easy to implement

- Costs very little

- Projected benefits are very high

Play around with the elements that could make your decision making effective for you. Between 3 and 5 elements is a good number to aim for.

Decision matrix

To put this all together and to make a useful tool you can construct a simple grid with these items at the top of the columns. An example of this is shown below, using the same criteria listed above:

Project	Appearance (A)	Ease (B)	Cost (C)	Benefits (D)	Total AxBxCxD
Scoring criteria	1 = -ve	1 = hard	1 = expensive	1 = no change	
	10 = very +ve	10 = very easy	10 = free	10 = huge change	
Examples					
New registration method	7	8	9	8	4032
New computer system	7	3	4	9	756

Once you have put in your opportunities you can score each element and then review the total scores. The higher the score the higher it should appear in your pile of things to do. The grid above is a little subjective, but it can give a better assessment of the opportunity list than using nothing at all.

Do it your way

Come up with your own ways of prioritising if the above method doesn't suit you. Providing a focus for your team as to what activity is going to be followed up and which ones aren't is important to keep the overall business improvement activity clear, focussed and maintaining its momentum. It is important that your team understand why their particular ideas are not going to be followed up. By having a clear priority system they can understand the reasoning behind the decision. One of the worst cases to have is to have people think that you are not interested in their ideas and consequently they stop providing you with new ideas.

One at a time

An additional point worth making is that it can become very easy to find a huge range of improvement opportunities during your discovery and analysis work. It is tempting to allocate each project to all of your available people, making them responsible for the project along with a deadline for completion. These are good things to do, but when you have a big long list of projects, taking a small section (prioritised of course) and then seeing that through to completion is more likely to get them all completed. When we have too many open projects it can become confusing, after all most people have day jobs to do on top of their improvement activities, let alone the tracking and remembering of what needs to be done next on a multitude of projects.
You will quickly find out what is the right level for your team to handle at any one time in order to achieve meaningful results. If you are in doubt though veer on the side of lower numbers and build up.

Summary

When we have too many improvement projects on our list of opportunities it can be daunting and difficult to manage. Developing a prioritisation method that can consistently determine what gets done next can make life easier for everyone involved and guarantees that the highest return on effort is achieved.

Action points

- Determine what characteristics would be associated with a great improvement project.

- Develop a system for evaluating each project so that you can rank it (such as the decision matrix above).

- Work down your project list in descending order of priority.

- Minimise / optimise the number of live projects to achieve an optimal balance of activity and delivering results.

Example: Missing the point

A client had been struggling with a rather large project that had numerous stakeholders, participants and sub-businesses all involved. Decisions had been made previously based on gut feel and hearsay. I would never play down gut feel, but as soon as a project decision was made it was retracted due to the amount of complaining that followed shortly afterwards.

To make life simple and fair we constructed a scoring method which was agreed by the stakeholders to be fair and effective. As soon as the scores were entered a clear plan of action was produced and the project began to gain momentum.

It is worth noting here that sometimes you need to work out what you are scoring to get a true reflection of what is important. For example, if you were trying to score something of a financial nature turnover might come to mind, where as profit would give you a different result. The same is true for quality errors. Measuring the number of errors instead of the cost of those errors would give you a different perspective again.

5 Why – Root Cause Problem Solving

One of the simplest tools to find out what is causing a problem is the 5 Why tool. It is so simple that many dismiss it altogether. If you have any experience of small children asking 'why?' repeatedly then you will understand how it works. Unfortunately this experience puts a lot of people off, but used correctly (and so as not to annoy your colleagues!) it can be quick and powerful.

To use the tool:
1. Identify a problem.
2. Ask 'why' it occurs.
3. State the answer.
4. Repeat steps 2 and 3 until you have an 'aha' moment, or a flash of the obvious (obvious now that you've stated it!)

The art of 5 Why is to ask meaningful questions that allow you to drill down. Just asking 'why' doesn't help the people you are working with to understand how to focus their thoughts. In some instances the more specific the better. Don't worry if this doesn't get you to a new level / insight. Just back up and ask a different 'why?' question.

Once you have reached a root cause situation it is useful to verify the logic of the sequence by joining the statements (in reverse from root cause up to effect) using 'so that'. If the logic of the statements don't flow then review the questions and the answers that are generated.

It's a simple tool, but it can provide some brilliant insights. If you solve the root cause problem then you could also solve a multitude of other problems that are manifesting within your business.

Action points

- Practice the '5 Why' technique until you consistently ask meaningful questions that get under the skin of the problem.

- Find root causes and then solve the issues that come up once and for all.

Example: 150 Problems

My first encounter with a client was being thrown into a conversation about the long list of over one hundred and fifty problems that their manufacturing function was facing. Rising to the challenge we used the 5 Why tool and drilled down to three fundamental issues that the business had neglected to deal with. We took a handful of other problems facing the business and immediately it was clear that all roads led back to the three issues discovered earlier.

The 5 why analysis took about five minutes and the issues that needed correcting were fully in the control of the business and fairly simple to rectify. Watching the change take place over the following two months was amazing. The myriad of problems that they had been pulling their hair out about were melting away and they were now able to get on with good old fashioned productive activity.

The client was incredibly sceptical about the tool because of its simplicity. The results changed their mind and it became one of their staple business improvement tools.

Simplifying Job Roles

Getting lost with work?

When a business is working at full tilt people's job roles can sometimes become blurred. Over time additional tasks get added and this can lead to the symptoms of poor time management and a lack of results. When we consider the mapped business process from earlier in the book this can make life simple for everyone involved with the process by (re)defining what the process is there to do. Jobs are just the same.

Purpose of a job

A quick way to define the purpose of the job is done by asking this question:
"how would a ten year old child describe what you do for a job?"
The answer needs to be less than five words and is usually something really simple. There will most likely be some resistance to this type of question as people have a lot of different and important responsibilities that they need to deliver. However, when we focus on improving the business process as our primary objective many of these behind the scenes activities can be prioritised accordingly. For those people

who genuinely do have a number of different hats to wear please see the sub-section on split roles below.

For someone who works in the purchasing function for example their answer might be "purchase raw materials". It's simple, but clear enough to make sure that our time is allocated to the right tasks.

Re-design the working day

If there are a number of different tasks that need to take place during the working day for a person on your team then splitting the day up into sections, or priorities, can help to get the maximum workload completed.

Based on the question "how would a ten year old child describe what you do for a job?" the primary purpose is most likely to be your first task of the day which could run until the work for that day is exhausted. Should that work be finished then the next most important task (or secondary purpose) that should be performed can be started. This is about improving the focus people have over their own roles.

Split roles

Of course it's not usually that straightforward and many people have a number of roles to perform. From a design point of view this could mean that the day would need to be split into clearly distinguishable parts. The reason for doing this is when one of roles takes more time than it should as one or more of the other roles doesn't get the time needed to deliver its results.

The quickest way to get around this is to create a time table, whether this runs daily, weekly or monthly. A simple example would be for someone who has two roles and they perform one role in the morning and one role in the afternoon. It allows a simplification of the working pattern, communicates with everyone what they will be doing when and gives that person the chance to do their job correctly.

The drip feeding of work into a role can create confusion and this can stop people from being able to juggle properly. They get stuck on one setting and the other roles come out sporadically as problems arise.

Daily cycles

However, sometimes the drip feeding, or responsiveness, needs to be a feature of the roles. Taking the last section a step further we have the option to create daily cycles that could mean (using the last section's example again) the following options can be created:

One Cycle
9am-12:30pm: Role 1
1pm-5pm: Role 2

Two Cycles
9am-11am: Role 1
11am-12:30pm: Role 2
1pm-3pm: Role 1
3pm-5pm: Role 2

Four Cycles
9am-10am: Role 1
10am-11am: Role 2
11am-12 noon: Role 1
12:30pm -1pm: Role 2
1pm-2pm: Role 1
2pm-3pm: Role 2
3pm-4pm: Role 1
4pm-5pm: Role 2

The tighter the cycles the greater the discipline required to stop what you are doing in one role and then move to another. However the tighter the schedule the better the access and responsiveness.

We can't fit the work into a day

Even after doing all of this you may find that the work just won't fit. If this is the case then it might be time to look at the way that the work is being conducted. Looking for ways to become more efficient is a good way to progress. So far we have looked at being more effective and delivering the internal service in an improved manner.

There are many quick ways to determine what can be improved, the simplest is to keep a time log of what happens during the working day. After only a couple of days you usually see a pattern of things happening that can be removed. Yes, the simplest improvement is to remove the things from the day that don't help. Making the remaining work content more efficient might involve your IT department, or some thinking away from the workplace, or working with another team to ensure that the work coming through is as simple as possible. This is a case of running through the six improvement steps again for the purpose of an individual's role.

Unnecessary meetings

As you reflect upon how your day is spent you may find that there are a number of meetings that are less than essential to your role. In fact there may be two ways to look at meetings that occur in your diary. One, you shouldn't be there. Two, the meeting takes too long. There are quick ways to get around these two issues.

If you can get out of the meetings then do so.

If meetings still need to take place why not challenge the business to conduct specific meetings in 15 minutes or less, putting the emphasis on decision making during the meeting. with information gathering and circulation taking place prior to the meeting. Schedule anything that cannot be resolved immediately for a separate get together.

Always use a timed agenda and log the actions.

Okay, some meetings won't be able to be squeezed down to under 15 minutes, but for the majority of meetings this is good target to go for. Make the meetings productive and useful. Meetings are so often an excuse to get out of work and this shouldn't be an option for your team.

Action steps

- Re-focus all staff members on their purpose.

- Re-design days for people who struggle with their time management, using split days / cycles as appropriate.

- Get the balance between routine and flexibility right in order for your team to generate results.

- Keep a time log and delete unnecessary activity wherever possible.

- Improve meetings by always using agendas, getting people to prepare properly and driving down the time available (off-lining things that need only some of the attendees to discuss after the meeting).

Example: The Buyer Buys

A business that I did some work for a few years ago had a number of staff members who did anything but their job!

The most memorable conversation was with a member of staff who worked in the Purchasing Department. The supply of materials into the business was behind schedule and the department generally was busy doing other things. When we redesigned how the business operation was going to work I asked one of the buyers what they were there to do. I got a long list of things, but not a clear crisp answer.

I asked this person to summarise their answer into five words or less, and we got to 'I buy materials to order'. Perfect.

Changing the operation was much easier when everyone was crystal clear about what their primary purpose was.

Summary

The book has been split into two main areas and has included the following principles.

Part One - Improvement Framework

Brand and Value

Know what is important to the business and to the customers so as to create a direction for making improvements.

Mapping

Know what needs to change by getting a map of the current situation.

Key Performance Indicators

Drive the performance of your business through having the right information in the right place at the right time.

Handovers

Remove the delays and mistakes between stages for big results.

Sales Intake

Ensure that the way that you accept work doesn't cripple the business.

Regulation

Optimise your resources by making sure things are happening the right way and through the control of your capacities.

Routines

Improve the discipline/regimen in the workplace for repeatable results.

Processes

Find the best way to do your work.

Part Two - Useful Tools

Continuous Improvement Matrix

Focus on a small part of the business and ideas can flow.

Kaizen

Use tiny steps to gain momentum, motivation and confidence.

PDCA

Come up with a good idea and then iterate it until it works brilliantly.

80/20

Some improvement activities will help a lot, some won't.

5 Why

Getting to the root of problems prevents them coming back!

Simplify Job Roles

Gist and purpose can improve clarity and raise effectiveness.

The Next Steps

We have now reached the end of the book.

From the sections that you have worked through I hope that you have found some ways to improve how your business works. I have aimed for a simple, cut through the nonsense approach, and I hope that you have found some ideas or approaches that have resonated with you.

Principles

All of the ideas in this book are based on principles. If your business doesn't seem to fit the profile of what we have talked about during the chapters then don't worry. It is the principle that matters and all it takes is a little bit of thinking about how it applies to your business. Many improvement approaches are not utilised because time is not spent working out how they can be applied to the business. I wish you success in being different and working out how these approaches can benefit your business, how they can make life easier for everyone in the business, and how they can give your customers better service at the same time.

Do it your way

It might take some time for the ideas to settle in your mind and for the opportunities to become obvious, but you have a chance to make the improvements happen in your own way. An observation you can make when you watch businesses try to improve is how they emulate other businesses who have already made significant improvements. Or, they find the next 'big thing' and try to implement that into their business hoping that this finally will be the solution to all of their troubles.

The businesses that are getting ahead aren't too worried about what you call a particular system or methodology, they *are* bothered about it working and the efforts being rewarded by higher levels of productivity, profits etc. Although this book is called *Business Process Re-engineering*, it really is about you creating a solid business system that you then improve over time. With that in mind, you might be wondering what the fastest way is to implement the changes you want in your business.

Talk

Get the people in your business talking about the objectives of the business. Keep talking about ideas on improving. Keep talking and asking for help if you can't get an improvement to work. Keep talking and challenging each other to raise your game. Keep talking to your customers and refining your services and products. Keep talking and learning so that you can do a better job. Keep talking and asking questions about the way that you do work now.

Make an ongoing conversation about 'doing it better' part of your business. Everyone knows something and might just need

that little bit of help to make things happen. That of course means that listening is crucial to making the talking part work.
If you want to accelerate progress keep the conversation flowing and keep everyone involved.

Results, modify, results

PDCA is a brilliant tool. At the end of the day all we want to see are the results. Sometimes we hit lucky and find a fast way to get something done. If we end up in a bit of a slog however and still aren't getting the results then don't give up. Stop, take stock and find a different approach. Measure your results and keep refining what you are doing. If a new approach works better and yields better results then switch. If you try something and it doesn't work then either refine it (PDCA) or go back to what was working and then come back and try again when you are ready.

Don't stop, keep moving in the direction you want to travel. There are enough tools and ideas in this book to keep you moving ahead for a long time.

Next

As we said at the start of this book there is a lot of information available on business improvement methods and techniques. There are advanced scheduling ideas, lead time reduction ideas, operations management ideas, ideas on everything. This book was designed to cut through the mist of ideas to give you a simple framework to launch your business improvement approach.

These ideas get results and in a short period of time too.

There is always more to learn, so once you have used this book and gained a boost in performance don't stop looking for ideas. The continuous improvement approach covered in this book should keep you going for a long time, but the more knowledge you have then the richer the resources you can draw upon to come up with the next improvement ideas.

Keep looking for the next improvement.

Enjoy!

Being able to improve your business is a great opportunity to stretch your mind and get a better relationship going with the other people in your business. When improvement starts to happen in a natural unforced way it can be a lot of fun.

It will take a lot of your time up so enjoy it. Seriously - it can be fun.

Action Point

- Take what you have learned and do something about it!

Compilation of Action Points

Action points from the previous sections of this book.

Cutting through the confusion

- Read the rest of the book!

- Start an ongoing conversation with your colleagues about improvement.

Brand and value

- Determine what value your business creates for its customers. Keep this as a focus for your improvements; we want to spend as much time on value adding work as possible.

- Compare your ideal brand with your current brand – where you want to be and where you are. All your changes need to help you move from your current brand to your ideal brand.

- Define some statements / principles for change to help you achieve your ideal way of working. Your changes need to help you adhere to your ideal brand and help your business to spend more time on value adding.

Mapping

- Identify your processes.

- Get your team together and list all of the steps and agree their sequence.

- List the gripes and obstacles that the process faces.

- Check the process steps with the 'because of' statement.

- Act upon the immediate ideas.

- Delete and merge steps that are obvious.

- Consider ideas for a total overhaul – as if you started all over again.

Key Performance Indicators

- Review the process map you have been working on and define the key steps in the process where specific achievements would allow improvement of the final results. For example, "paperwork completed on time at the sales order processing stage".

- Identify the 'digital' tasks that need to be included. These are the 'yes' or 'no' questions that can help to decide if a function has operated in accordance with its purpose in the business.

- Decide how the information that you can gain from these KPIs could be used and manipulate its form until a meaningful measure is achieved.

- Review the list of KPIs and consider the people and functions in your business to see if a concise but all encompassing list has been achieved.

- Pre-define the corrective actions that need to take place when specific KPI performances have been 'breached'.

Handovers

- Review your process map for the business and chunk it into groups based on departments / teams.

- Identify each handover step / action and find out what happens.

- Learn what should ideally happen at the handover to minimise delays, errors, frustrations etc. and re-design the activity.

- Look out for in-trays or piles of work building up just after the handover, and if necessary class this as part of the handover and get to work on it.

- Use this opportunity to improve the working relationships between functions in your business (or even your supply chain) by learning about each other and improving each other's working lives.

Sales intake and regulation

- Create an acceptance procedure for your business and use this as a meeting agenda (or a checklist for an individual) when letting new orders into your business.

- Do not let any orders into your business without them passing the contract review stage.

- Develop simple capacity tools to allow you to gauge work content entering your business.

- Periodically (weekly, for example) smooth and adjust your schedules based on the work already done and the work scheduled to start so that your resources are optimised and that your customer gets what they want when they want it.

Discipline and routines

- Review your map and identify the key tasks that are at cause that need to happen like clockwork.

- Create a time table for your business that everyone agrees to.

- Work with individuals to create checklists or personal time tables as appropriate to overcome (internal) delivery problems.

- Link this work with the section on 'regulation'.

Regulation of resources

- Identify the critical points in the process.

- Create 'killer questions'.

- Create a daily (Sunrise) meeting and help all functions to help each other.

- Implement a monthly S&OP type meeting where the progress of each function is considered against the business plan, and adjust activity accordingly.

- Create a few scenarios that could happen to your business and define how (and who) the business would need to operate should the scenario occur.

Improving your processes

- Chunk your processes from your map of the business processes and prioritise what needs doing.

- Get a team together who have different points of views / skills.

- Walk through a process using the worksheets and observe and question – but don't judge yet.

- Collate all of the findings and then judge.

- Find out the root causes of the concerns and create solutions to remedy the concerns.

- Chip away at the improvements, a little every week is better than a big blowout followed by nothing at all.

- Keep going until the process is 'slick'.

- Diarise a date for the next session of improvement for this process.

- Move to the next process that you have prioritised.

Effective continuous improvement

- Split your business down into tasks / processes.

- Define how your business could improve - "factors".

- Create the continuous improvement matrix.

- Get a team together and use the described agenda to start generating ideas.

- Implement the ideas, complete the matrix and then repeat.

Getting things moving

- Find a way to keep an ongoing conversation about the improvements that need to take place. A weekly meeting, a daily chat - whatever works for you and your team.

- Find stalled projects and break the first few steps (until the first milestone?) into tiny steps.

- If you come up against any form of inertia then consider tiny steps the whole way. At least the project will conclude - better at a slower pace than not at all.

Experiment and make progress

- Share the PDCA tool with your team.

- Apply PDCA to all of your business improvement activities.

- Create an improvement tracking spreadsheet that incorporates the elements of Plan Do Check Act, in a way that makes sense to you.

Prioritisation

- Determine what characteristics would be associated with a great improvement project.

- Develop a system for evaluating each project so that you can rank it.

- Work down your project list in descending order of priority.

- Minimise / optimise the number of live projects to achieve an optimal balance of activity and delivering results.

5 Why

- Practice the '5 Why' technique until you consistently ask meaningful questions that get under the skin of the problem.

- Find root causes and then solve the issues that come up once and for all.

Simplifying job roles

- Re-focus all staff members on their purpose.

- Re-design days for people who struggle with their time management, using split days / cycles as appropriate.

- Get the balance between routine and flexibility right in order for your team to generate results.

- Keep a time log and delete unnecessary activity where possible.

- Improve meetings by always using agendas, getting people to prepare properly and driving down the time available (off-lining things that need only some of the attendees to discuss after the meeting).

Links and Resources

Smartspeed Blog

For more ideas on how to improve your business and to find out how to apply some of the more common business improvement ideas in novel ways please visit our blog:

www.smartspeed.info

Free On Time Delivery Report

If you want some ideas around improving the on time delivery performance of your business, then please download our free report. You will need to register your email address on our website, the link is:

www.smartspeed.co.uk

LinkedIn OTIF Forum

If you would like to join us online to discuss practical ideas around improving on time delivery performance then please visit our LinkedIn group:

http://www.linkedin.com/groups/On-Time-Delivery-Improvement-4419220/about

'Making It Happen' Programme

Discover practical change management strategies with this 52 week online course, aimed at accelerating the rate of change at your place of work.

www.systemsandprocesses.co.uk

About Giles Johnston

Giles is a Chartered Engineer with a background in Operations Management who spends most of his time working on capacity planning and 'on time delivery' improvement projects.

He has worked in a variety of different roles within manufacturing prior to working as a consultant for a prestigious university.

In 2005 Giles decided to forge his own path and created Smartspeed, which has been helping businesses to improve their delivery performance, along with their profits, ever since.

Giles can be contacted by:
Email -   **gilesjohnston@smartspeed.co.uk**
Website -   **www.smartspeed.co.uk**

Smartspeed's Contact Details

Thank you for purchasing this book, if you have any comments we would love to read them.

(w) www.smartspeed.co.uk

(t) +44 191 645 3086

(e) info@smartspeed.co.uk

For information about our other products and consulting services please get in touch using the details above.

Made in the USA
Middletown, DE
11 April 2017